# "Eh ... Jesus ..."
# "Yes, Peter ... ?"
# Book 3

## CONTENTS

Introduction ..............................Page 3
SQUARE ONE.................................. 4
IMMACULATE................................. 6
WATER OR WINE?........................... 8
GOING UNDER............................. 10
IN GOD'S IMAGE.......................... 12
F.T. INDEX..................................... 14
SOPHISTICATION ........................ 16

John Bell and Graham Maule are members of the Iona Community and lead the Wild Goose Worship Group.

First Published 1990

Dedicated to the

organisers and participants

of

GREENBELT FESTIVALS

with

gratitude and affection.

®™

The Wild Goose is a Celtic symbol of the Holy Spirit.
It serves as the Trademark of Wild Goose Publications

## WILD GOOSE PUBLICATIONS
The Publishing Division of The Iona Community

Pearce Institute, 840 Govan Road, GLASGOW G51 3UT
Tel.(041) 445 4561  —  Fax.(041) 445 4295

© **1990 The Iona Community**     **ISBN 0 947988 43 2**

Printed by Coubrough & McKeracher (Printers) Limited, Glasgow G5 8HL

# Introduction

The popularity of the last two Peter and Jesus books has encouraged us to produce a third. But, as before, the scripts do not come out of a vacuum, but out of real situations in which we have been asked to lead worship.

*WATER OR WINE?* was prepared for the 1990 Christian Aid Festival in Coventry which had its title 'All Things New.' *SOPHISTICATION* was written for an annual Polytechnic church service.

The others, or most of them, owe their genesis to GREENBELT FESTIVALS at which we have been privileged to work for several years. The encouragement of the organisers and the receptiveness of the participants have been a continual source of inspiration as well as a stretching experience. To all of them we are glad to dedicate this third book.

John L. Bell
Graham Maule
October 1990

# Square One

| | | |
|---|---|---|
| PETER | : | Eh . . . Jesus? |
| JESUS | : | Yes, Peter? |
| PETER | : | How do you manage to sleep? |
| JESUS | : | I put my head on a pillow and I close my eyes. |
| PETER | : | And then what? |
| JESUS | : | And then I go to sleep. |
| PETER | : | Just like that? |
| JESUS | : | Just like that. |
| PETER | : | You don't count sheep and goats or drink hot camel's milk? |
| JESUS | : | No. |
| PETER | : | What about that time with the *Maid of Galilee* ? |
| JESUS | : | Don't listen to rumours, Peter. |
| PETER | : | No . . . that's my father's fishing boat. Remember how we went out in it and a storm blew up and you just lay there snoring? |
| JESUS | : | Do I snore, Peter? |
| PETER | : | (EXASPERATED) Jesus, the point is not whether or not you snore. How did you manage to sleep? |
| JESUS | : | I put my head on a pillow and closed my eyes. |
| PETER | : | So we're back to square one. |
| JESUS | : | No, Peter, we've actually arrived at the whole point of this conversation. |
| PETER | : | But, Jesus, you've avoided the issue ! |
| JESUS | : | Not at all, Peter. You've avoided the issue. The issue is not how I manage to sleep, but the fact that you don't. You don't really want to ask me about my sleeping habits. You want to tell me about yours . . . right? (SILENCE) Right? |
| PETER | : | (SHEEPISHLY) Right. Jesus, I'm not sleeping very well. I mean . . . I just can't get to sleep. |

4

| | | |
|---|---|---|
| JESUS | : | What about counting sheep and goats and drinking hot milk? |
| PETER | : | No . . .<br>I remember when I was a boy<br>how I could never get to sleep.<br>I used to be so excited about what was<br>going to happen tomorrow.<br><br>I'd lie awake wondering what new thing was going to happen, wondering whether my father would take us . . . |
| JESUS | : | And now? |
| PETER | : | And now I lie awake worrying about tomorrow<br>and afraid of what might be in front of us.<br><br>And then I watch you sleeping,<br>and hear you snoring,<br>and I don't know how you can do it. |
| JESUS | : | Peter,<br>can we go back a wee bit.<br>You say that you never worried about tomorrow<br>when you were a boy.<br><br>Did you never worry that you might get caught in a storm<br>or that your boat might get lost in the darkness? |
| PETER | : | No, I never thought about that. |
| JESUS | : | Why not? |
| PETER | : | Because I knew my father would be there. |
| JESUS | : | Now you know how I've managed to sleep . . . |
| PETER | : | What do you mean? |
| JESUS | : | Peter,<br><br>God is in tomorrow<br>a long time before we are.<br>Let him do the worrying and you do the sleeping. |
| PETER | : | And what about saying your prayers? |
| JESUS | : | If you want to pray, then pray.<br>But don't make it a time to count your worries.<br>Just recognise who is in control, and trust him.<br><br>(PAUSE) |
| JESUS | : | So . . .<br>enjoy your sleep when you can.<br><br>That way you might be ready<br>when I need you to stay awake. |

* * * * * * *

**5**

# Immaculate

| | | |
|---|---|---|
| JESUS | : | Eh, Peter . . . ? |
| PETER | : | Yes, Jesus? |
| JESUS | : | Did I see you giggling just now when I was speaking to the Pharisees? |
| PETER | : | No. |
| JESUS | : | Peter, my eyes don't deceive me.<br>You were giggling when I was speaking to the Pharisees. |
| PETER | : | I wasn't giggling when you were speaking to the Pharisees.<br>I started giggling when you were speaking to the lawyers. |
| JESUS | : | Why? |
| PETER | : | Jesus, you should have seen yourself.<br>You were immaculate.<br><br>There you were laying into the Pharisees,<br>telling them that they didn't know the first thing about justice,<br>   — that they were religious show-offs . . . . |
| JESUS | : | (INTERRUPTING) Did I say that? |
| PETER | : | Well you said they loved seats of honour in the synagogue . . .<br>it's one and the same thing.<br><br>Then you accused them of being unmarked graves, and all the time the lawyers were smirking to themselves in a corner.<br><br>And then this upstart thought he'd mix it a bit and said that he found your language insulting.<br><br>But the last thing he expected was that you'd turn on him and give him a dose of the same medicine right between the eyes. |
| JESUS | : | (INTERRUPTING) . . . Peter . . . |
| PETER | : | (OBLIVIOUS). . Oh Jesus you really gave them laldie.(or what for)<br>You should have seen yourself . . .<br>You grew about six inches taller<br>and your eyes fixed him in your stare<br>and your voice went all quiet and husky:<br><br>(MIMICKING) "You lawyers . . it's no better for you.<br>You load people with intolerable burdens<br>and you don't lift a finger to help them carry their load. . ." |
| JESUS | : | (INTERRUPTING) . Peter . . . |
| PETER | : | (OBLIVIOUS) "You've stolen the key to the house of knowledge.<br>You can't go in yourselves and you make sure nobody else will enter.<br><br>You build tombs . . ." |
| JESUS | : | (INTERRUPTING) Peter . . . Peter . . . |
| PETER | : | Jesus, I was just coming to the good bit. |
| JESUS | : | For a lousy fishermen, you make a good actor. |

| PETER | : | But, Jesus . . . you were immaculate.<br>You wiped the floor with them.<br>I felt like passing round the smelling salts . . .<br>they were like jelly. |
|---|---|---|
| JESUS | : | Well I must admit they did seem a bit shaken. |
| PETER | : | Shaken?? . . Don't sell yourself short, Jesus.<br>They were decimated !<br>Did you intend it that way? |
| JESUS | : | Well, Peter, unlike you . .<br>I didn't rehearse my words.<br>It wasn't till I began that I knew what I had to say. |
| PETER | : | You mean . . . all that . . . just came out? |
| JESUS | : | Yes. |
| PETER | : | Immaculate ! |
| JESUS | : | Is that this week's 'in' word? |
| PETER | : | But if it just came to you without any rehearsal,<br>it was immaculate. |
| JESUS | : | Well if you say so. |
| PETER | : | Is it always like that, Jesus?<br>Do you never prepare what you are going to say? |
| JESUS | : | Oh, sometimes.<br>If I'm going to tell a story I go over it in my mind,<br>so I know what follows.<br>But in any case, Peter,<br>all of my life is a preparation for what I'm going to say.<br><br>All the things I hear in the street,<br>all the people who tell me their secrets,<br>all the reflecting or arguing about what the Bible says . . .<br>that's all preparation. |
| PETER | : | But how come you know exactly what to say when your<br>back's against the wall . . . like with the Pharisees? |
| JESUS | : | Peter, sometimes it's not until your back's against the wall<br>that you know what to say or discover the truth.<br><br>If you avoid controversy,<br>if you speak only to those who agree with you,<br>you never discover the new things God has to teach you. |
| PETER | : | Even when you're arguing with the Pharisees? |
| JESUS | : | Even when you're arguing with the Pharisees. |
| PETER | : | (PAUSE) Jesus . . . were you annoyed when I mimicked you? |
| JESUS | : | No. I found it quite amusing,<br>but very glad that you remember what I say. |

* * * * * * *

7

# Water Or Wine?

PETER    :  Eh . . . Jesus . . . ?

JESUS    :  Yes, Peter.

PETER    :  What would you rather have . . .
a glass of water or a glass of wine?

JESUS    :  Who's buying?

PETER    :  Never mind who's buying, which would you prefer?

JESUS    :  I'm not thirsty . . .

PETER    :  But . . . if you were thirsty . . .

JESUS    :  It would depend on the time of day and where I was.

PETER    :  What do you mean?

JESUS    :  Well, if it was nine o'clock in the morning and
I was in the middle of a class of school children,
it wouldn't be wine.

PETER    :  Because it's alcoholic?

JESUS    :  No . . .
because I don't know many schools that have a bar in them.
But what is all this talk about wine anyway?

PETER    :  It's not me that talks about wine.

JESUS    :  That's right. You don't talk about it.
You conduct an interrogation . . . Why?

PETER    :  To test the strength of your interest.

JESUS    :  Oh I see . . .
You're surveying the potential market before you
open an off sales. Is that it?

PETER    :  No . . . people are just talking again.

JESUS    :  Are they calling me an alcoholic?

PETER    :  How did you know?

JESUS    :  Well it wouldn't surprise me.
If I talk to a girl at the side of the road,
        I get called a womaniser.
If I heal a centurion's servant,
        they call me a military sympathiser.
If I as much as smile at a Pharisee,
        I'm a pawn of the establishment.

So if I take a glass of wine,
        I'm bound to be called an alcoholic.

PETER    :  Does it not bother you?

| | | |
|---|---|---|
| JESUS | : | Not really, Peter. |
| | | I mean, it's a no-win situation. |
| | | If I refused a drink, I'd be called a kill-joy. |
| | | If I accept a glass, I'm a total inebriate. |
| | | There's no pleasing everybody. |
| PETER | : | You could wear a temperance badge on one lapel and a real ale badge on the other. |
| JESUS | : | No, Peter . . . that's the kind of thing you would do. |
| | | I prefer not to give significance to such a minor issue. |
| PETER | : | But do you not think you should be showing an example? |
| JESUS | : | Well, there's two things, Peter. |
| | | The first is that I live in Palestine and |
| | | wine is our national drink. |
| | | If I lived in Turkey, I'd probably drink coffee and get labelled a caffeine addict. |
| | | And secondly, wine is all right for me, |
| | | but it might be all wrong for other people. |
| | | And I want to respect and be sensitive to that. |
| | | I don't believe that me taking a glass of wine will make other people alcoholic, if that's what you are implying. |
| | | But if I were to get drunk . . . |
| | | that would be another matter. |
| PETER | : | All right, but even in your stories, you mention drink. |
| JESUS | : | I do? |
| PETER | : | What about the man who built a winepress? |
| JESUS | : | Peter . . . that's local industry and I'm a local person. |
| | | All my stories are about things people can identify with. |
| | | It would be pointless talking about micro-technology and thermodynamics to people who know nothing about them. |
| PETER | : | . . . thermo what ? ? |
| JESUS | : | Exactly ! |
| PETER | : | (PAUSE) . . . What about putting new wine in new skins? |
| JESUS | : | What about it? When I talked about that I wasn't giving a lesson in home-brewing, |
| | | I was using something that people know about to let them into the secrets of the Kingdom of Heaven. |
| PETER | : | All right. You've convinced me. |
| | | Are you feeling thirsty now? |
| JESUS | : | I am. |
| PETER | : | What would you like . . . water or wine? |
| JESUS | : | It's my round, Peter . . . what would you like? |

\* \* \* \* \* \* \*

**9**

# In God's Image

PETER   :  Eh . . . Jesus . . .

JESUS   :  Yes, Peter?

PETER   :  Do you know how it says in the Bible
that God made man and woman in his own image?

JESUS   :  Yes.

PETER   :  Is that true?

JESUS   :  Yes . . . why?

PETER   :  Well . . . men and women are . . .
not the same . . . they're . . . you know . . . different.

JESUS   :  Is this a sex education lesson, Peter?

PETER   :  No . . . . I just can't understand how men and women
can be like God if they're not like each other.

JESUS   :  But, Peter,
you look very like your sisters.
I've seen them . . . they have the same kind of hair as you,
they have the same black eyes,
they have the same small nose.

PETER   :  Yes . . . but not all parts are the same.

JESUS   :  I admit that.

PETER   :  But never mind men and women.
Not all men are the same.

Some men are very tall,
some are fat.
Some have a lot of hair,
some are bald.
Some have black skins,
some have white skins.

JESUS   :  (MIMICKING) Some never speak,
some never shut up.

PETER   :  (A LITTLE TAKEN ABACK)
. . . Yes . . .
are they all made in God's image?

JESUS   :  Yes.

PETER   :  What about a blind man with only one leg,
is he made in God's image?

JESUS   :  Yes.

PETER   :  What about a woman with no teeth
and big ears,
is she made in God's image?

| | | |
|---|---|---|
| JESUS | : | Yes. |
| PETER | : | What about a baby dying of hunger, is it made in God's image? |
| JESUS | : | Yes. |
| PETER | : | What about . . ? |
| JESUS | : | (INTERRUPTING) Peter, Peter, that's enough. |
| PETER | : | But I'm just trying to point out that everybody is different. There are no two people the same. |
| JESUS | : | Exactly. That's what it means to be made in God's image |

JESUS :
There is only one God.
God is unique.
And the people who God makes
are all, like him, unique.

| | | |
|---|---|---|
| PETER | : | But what about the people who are evil? What about the people who abuse children, or terrorists who bomb innocent civilians? |

Surely they're not made in God's image?

| | | |
|---|---|---|
| JESUS | : | Yes, they are. |
| PETER | : | But, Jesus ! |
| JESUS | : | But, Peter . . . to be unique is not the same as to be good. |

God makes us all unique
and he loves us all uniquely.
But whether we are good or bad is up to us.

| | | |
|---|---|---|
| PETER | : | But what about the starving child? |
| JESUS | : | The starving child is also made in God's image. The starving child is also unique. |

And perhaps only when people appreciate the value
of each individual life,
there will be no more starving children
. . . for all will be fed;
and perhaps no more criminals,
because they will have been loved.

| | | |
|---|---|---|
| PETER | : | Do you never wish that people weren't so different? Would it not be easier if some were the same? |
| JESUS | : | Do you mean would I like two of you? |
| PETER | : | Well, perhaps, Jesus. |
| JESUS | : | Definitely not, Peter. |

\* \* \* \* \* \* \*

# F.T. Index

| | | |
|---|---|---|
| PETER | : | Eh . . . . Jesus? |
| JESUS | : | Yes, Peter? |
| PETER | : | I've just been looking at the crowd. |
| JESUS | : | Aha . . . . and . . . ? |
| PETER | : | . . . and there's a lot of F.T.'s about today. |
| JESUS | : | What's an F.T., Peter?<br>I was never very good at acronyms. |
| PETER | : | Pharisee Types. |
| JESUS | : | (PAUSE)<br>Pharisee Types? |
| PETER | : | Uhuh. I've counted at least 29. |
| JESUS | : | It's not your arithmetic I want to dispute, Peter . .<br>it's your spelling.<br>Pharisee is spelt with a P, not an F. |
| PETER | : | Make allowances, Jesus.<br>I'm just an illiterate fisherman . . . remember? |
| JESUS | : | Well, that's your story.<br>But tell me, why are you worried about the Pharisees? |
| PETER | : | Because they're on the increase . . .<br>I mean, when we started with you,<br>we never saw them,<br>except when we went into a synagogue or the Temple.<br>And they certainly never came looking for us.<br>You were beneath their contempt,<br>but now it's a different story. |
| JESUS | : | Peter, to some extent that has to be expected.<br>Wherever there is the possibility of good,<br>there's also the potential for evil.<br><br>The more we . . . and I mean all of us . . .<br>preach or teach or heal<br>we have to expect criticism and confrontation.<br>The Gospel is a threat to the status quo,<br>not its friend<br>and certainly not its sanctifier. |
| PETER | : | But, Jesus,<br>there are more and more of them,<br>and they've got influence . . .<br>influential friends in high places<br>and dicey friends in low places.<br>And they've got power. |

| | | |
|---|---|---|
| JESUS | : | And you haven't? |
| PETER | : | Jesus . . . my name used to be Simon . . . not Samson. |
| JESUS | : | Let me tell you, Peter . . .<br>if you were a candle, . . . just a wee light . . .<br>all the darkness in the world couldn't put you out.<br>And you, small as you were,<br>would have more power than all the darkness. |
| PETER | : | (IMPATIENTLY)<br>Yes, Jesus . . . but I'm not a candle. |
| JESUS | : | Yes, I know that.<br>But if you are, as you say, an illiterate fisherman,<br>and my Spirit lives in you,<br>then that will be more powerful<br>than all the Pharisees and their lackeys put together. |
| PETER | : | Well, I'm not so sure about that. |
| JESUS | : | Well, be sure about this,<br>that the people to fear — if you must fear the powerful —<br>are not those who look threatening and would harm you.<br><br>Fear, rather, those who seem friendly<br>but who do nothing.<br><br>The biggest threat to the Gospel is not those who are<br>obviously bad<br>but those who are willingly apathetic . . . |
| PETER | : | Well, Jesus, I know how to spot the Pharisee Types,<br>but how do you spot the apathetics? |
| JESUS | : | I'm not telling you. |
| PETER | : | Why not? |
| JESUS | : | Because your job is not just to be on the defence against evil<br>but to be on the attack with the good. |
| PETER | : | Jesus . . . that's very military language. |
| JESUS | : | Sorry, Peter . . . it must be seeing the centurions in the<br>crowd. |
| PETER | : | Are you sure they're centurions? |
| JESUS | : | Why, what do you think they are? |
| PETER | : | Pharisees in fancy dress. |

\* \* \* \* \* \* \*

# CURRENT PUBLICATIONS OF THE IONA COMMUNITY

THE WHOLE EARTH SHALL CRY GLORY (Paperback)     ISBN 0 947988 00 9
THE WHOLE EARTH SHALL CRY GLORY (Hardback)     ISBN 0 947988 04 1
*Iona prayers by Rev. George F. MacLeod*
THE IONA COMMUNITY WORSHIP BOOK     ISBN 0 947988 28 9
*Iona Community*
THE CORACLE — Rebuilding The Common Life     ISBN 0 947988 25 4
*Jubilee reprint of Foundation Documents of the Iona Community*
RE-INVENTING THEOLOGY     ISBN 0 947988 29 7
*Ian M. Fraser*
PARABLES AND PATTER     ISBN 0 947988 33 5
*Erik Cramb*
ROGER — An Extraordinary Peace Campaigner     ISBN 0 947988 38 6
*Helen Steven*
LIVING A COUNTERSIGN — From Iona To Basic Christian Communities ISBN 0 947988 39 4
*Ian Fraser*
HEAVEN SHALL NOT WAIT (Wild Goose Songs Volume 1)     ISBN 0 947988 23 8
*John Bell & Graham Maule*
ENEMY OF APATHY (Wild Goose Songs Volume 2)     ISBN 0 947988 27 0
*John Bell & Graham Maule*
LOVE FROM BELOW (Wild Goose Songs Volume 3)     ISBN 0 947988 34 3
*John Bell & Graham Maule*
LOVE FROM BELOW (Cassette)     No.IC/WGP/008
*Wild Goose Worship Group*
CLOTH FOR THE CRADLE (Cassette)     No.IC/WGP/007
*Wild Goose Worship Group*
A TOUCHING PLACE (Cassette)     No.IC/WGP/004
*Wild Goose Worship Group*
FOLLY AND LOVE (Cassette)     No.IC/WGP/005
*Iona Abbey*
FREEDOM IS COMING (Cassette)     No.IC/WGP/006
FREEDOM IS COMING     ISBN 0 947988 49 1
*Utryck*
MANY AND GREAT (World Church Songs - Volume 1)     ISBN 0 947988 40 8
*John Bell & Graham Maule*
MANY AND GREAT (Cassette)     IC/WGP/009
*Wild Goose Worship Group*
PRAISING A MYSTERY     ISBN 0 947988 36 X
*Brian Wren*
BRING MANY NAMES     ISBN 0 947988 37 8
*Brian Wren*
WILD GOOSE PRINTS No. 1     ISBN 0 947988 06 8
*John Bell & Graham Maule*
WILD GOOSE PRINTS No. 2     ISBN 0 947988 10 6
*John Bell & Graham Maule*
WILD GOOSE PRINTS No. 3     ISBN 0 947988 24 6
*John Bell & Graham Maule*
WILD GOOSE PRINTS No. 4     ISBN 0 947988 35 1
*John Bell & Graham Maule*
WILD GOOSE PRINTS No. 5     ISBN 0 947988 41 6
*John Bell & Graham Maule*
WILD GOOSE PRINTS No. 6     ISBN 0 947988 42 4
*John Bell & Graham Maule*
EH... JESUS... YES, PETER...? Book 1     ISBN 0 947988 20 3
*John Bell & Graham Maule*
EH... JESUS... YES, PETER...? Book 2     ISBN 0 947988 31 9
*John Bell & Graham Maule*
EH... JESUS... YES, PETER...? Book 3     ISBN 0 947988 43 2
*John Bell & Graham Maule*
WHAT IS THE IONA COMMUNITY?     ISBN 0 947988 07 6
*Iona Community*
CO-OPERATION VERSUS EXPLOITATION     ISBN 0 947988 22 X
*Walter Fyfe*
COLUMBA     ISBN 0 947988 11 4
*Mitchell Bunting*
FEEL IT — Detached Youth Work In Action     ISBN 0 947988 32 7
*Cilla McKenna*